THE TERROR OF HELL

Published by Revival Nation Publishing

ISBN 978-1-926625-15-7

Cover design by John Burton
www.johnburtondesign.com

Printed in the United States of America

Revival Nation Publishing
Ontario • CANADA

P.O. Box 30001
RPO Eastland Plaza
Sarnia, Ontario
N7T 0A7

www.RevivalNationPublishing.com
1-866-487-1361

To my family. We're passionate about God now, and we'll enjoy Him together forever in eternity.

John and Amy Burton planted Revolution House of Prayer in Manitou Springs, Colorado in 2001. This ministry of intercession, warfare, and strategic Kingdom advance is the first piece of the puzzle in what will ultimately be a region-wide revival.

In 1991 John received an life-changing assignment from God to see an entire city set free. Over the years, God added to that vision and has since revealed that his dream is to see Manitou Springs transformed into an entire city that ministers to God 24- hours a day. That launched the Revolution team into a fresh season as a house of prayer, a house of worship and a house of dreams for the Pikes Peak region and way, way beyond!

John's ministry style could be described as wildly passionate, engaging, humorous and loaded with the flow and power of the Holy Spirit.

The prevailing theme of the ministry God has given John revolves around the topic of 'being with God'. Where God is, things happen. In his presence, the place where he is, is the fullness of joy. As we discover the wonderful mystery of walking in the Spirit, praying always and making aggressive strides in faith, life becomes incredible!

It truly is an experience in the invisible realm. As we tangibly experience God through deep and active prayer we are interacting 'in the Spirit'. As we walk by faith and understand how amazing a Holy Spirit driven life is, being a believer quickly becomes the greatest adventure on earth!

If you would like to invite John to speak at your church, conference, camp or other event please visit www.johnburton.net.

THE TERROR OF HELL
by
JOHN BURTON

.

I'M GOING TO HELL?
THAT'S IMPOSSIBLE!

How could I be going to hell? What I was experiencing messed with my theology to a radically uncomfortable degree. The Holy Spirit was making sure I would never be the same again. Mission accomplished.

I count the early 1990's as the most significant season of my life to date. God had invaded my life. The Holy Spirit took me beyond a mere acceptance of Jesus as savior to a place of breath-taking experience in his 'invisible realm'. The suddenly all-consuming desire of my heart was to 'be with God' every moment of my life. I was craving and experiencing a legitimate, reportable and constantly weighty manifestation of the presence of God in my life. The desire and the cry of my heart was, "More!"

In those early years, many things happened that I'll never forget- but one event shook me like no other before or since.

I had a dream.

I was living in an old, vacant church building as the care taker. My massive 5'7" 150 pound frame must have been quite threatening to any would-be intruder! I had spent many hours praying in this empty building alone as the Lord was forming me in some very memorable ways. One night I laid down for bed as I did every other night. Nothing seemed out of the ordinary. I prayed myself to sleep as I had done so many times before.

What was about to happen as I slipped into sleep that fateful night would change me. Forever. In fact, because of the terror I experienced that night, the next thirteen years I would often pray as I went to sleep, "God, please don't give me any dreams tonight."

Thirteen years! God eventually spoke clearly to me, after thirteen years of receiving many visions, but no dreams of God, "John, I need you to stop praying that prayer. I have things to reveal to you. I need to talk to you. I have dreams for you to dream." I repented and have since craved dreams, angelic visitations and other forms of communication from the heavenly realm.

During this night of terror I fell asleep in the old church building and found myself dreaming.

In my dream I was laying on my stomach in a one room building. It was very comfortable inside, though there was nothing in the room. It was empty. I laid on the carpet and looked out of the two windows, one in front of me and one to my right. The overwhelming feeling that I had was one of comfort and relaxation. I had no concerns and no thoughts beyond enjoying the atmosphere I was in.

Through the windows I could see a beautiful sunny day unfolding. The trees were blowing in a gentle breeze. The birds were chirping and flying from tree to tree. I couldn't have asked for a better afternoon.

Then I experienced a changing of the scene. Like time lapse photography, I saw the atmosphere suddenly change. The clouds were ever so slightly darkening and increasing in coverage in the sky. The gentle breeze picked up velocity and the sky was a bit darker as the sun was hidden beyond the clouds. It seemed as if some rain may be moving in. I laid there and watched it unfold and remained immersed in my own comfort. I was taking deep breaths and enjoying every moment of my day.

Time lapsed again and I saw the sky completely covered in clouds- clouds much darker than just a few moments ago. I could smell the rain coming. The birds were taking cover as the wind picked up significantly. In the distance I saw several lightning strikes. It sure seemed as if this could be quite a storm. I was feeling great in my small one room shack. I stretched out and relaxed even more. What a wonderful day I was having.

Again, I watched the scene change suddenly. Now, it was quite obvious the storm would most definitely hit. The wind was intense and the rain started to hit the windows. Lightning struck less than 300 yards away and hail could be heard hitting the roof. It was time for concern, but I didn't feel any. I laid there, just as I did when it was a beautiful sunny day, and enjoyed the safety of my environment. I was feeling so good.

One more time, time lapsed and I found myself at ground zero. The storm of the century was upon me. The massive trees were nearly snapping in two as they bent over parallel to the ground. The hail was massive in size and was slamming every surface around me. The windows were buckling in and out as the incredible pressure of the storm weighed on them. The lightning was literally striking mere feet from the shack. The walls were shaking. You can imagine what I was experiencing in that terrible moment- beautiful peace, safety and comfort. It truly was a wonderful day, until-

In a fraction of a moment my overwhelming sense of peace and safety and relaxation turned to the most gripping terror I had ever known. It was as if every source of life and good had been eliminated from the atmosphere. Evil dominated the place that just moments ago was so enjoyable.

My mind raced in an attempt to figure out what had just happened. The fear I was experiencing was beyond description. It made no sense.

Suddenly, as I laid there on my stomach, two hands grabbed my ankles. My terror escalated to levels I cannot describe. I quickly looked back and saw nothing- but I knew a demonic entity had grabbed on to me.

The grip on my ankles was like a vice. I could not escape. My life, which seemingly just moments ago had been under my own control, was now in the control of an invisible yet very powerful force. A force that I knew had intents to destroy me.

Again, the terror immediately increased nearly to the point of literally losing control of my mind as that demon started to pull me backwards- and then down. Down into the floor of that shack. I knew I was going to Hell.

How can this be? It's impossible! I'm going to Hell? But, I'm 'saved'. I accepted Jesus as my Lord and Savior. This is contrary to everything I have ever learned in church. Yet, the moment was real, and I was losing every ounce of hope. I was about to enter an eternity of continual torture.

The demon kept pulling me downward. My feet were well below the floor and my waist was at ground level. Suddenly my hope increased. I thought to myself, "If I say the name of 'Jesus', the demon must flee!"

So, in my new state of hope I was able to squeeze out, "In the name of J-----. Ahhhhh! In the name of J-----."

I couldn't say it! The demon was controlling my very breath. I was suffocating every time that name was about to be said. I could have said any word in the dictionary- but that one. My hope instantly was lost and I started to cry out as I tremored under the control of that demon.

He continued to pull me down. My neck and then my mouth were entering hell as my body was taken below. At the height of my terror, and as my eyes were about to descend beneath the floor, I woke up.

I sat straight up in my bed. I was sweating in such volume that my entire bed was saturated. The light switch was no more than 7 feet from my bed. Just two quick steps to the wall would have been all it took to lighten the room. But I was frozen. I sat there for at least 3 hours in the darkness in absolute terror.

I finally fell back to sleep and awoke the next morning. I looked outside the two windows that were there in my bedroom in that old church building. It was a beautiful sunny day- but I did not feel comfortable or relaxed. I was shaken.

I begged God to tell me why I had that dream. What had just happened? Finally, later on that day, He spoke to me, "John, you represented the church. You were comfortable in your place of supposed safety. The storm was intensifying yet you were lulled into a state of apathy. Many in the church will be surprised one day, just as you were surprised in the dream, to find themselves under the control of demons as they are taken to hell."

> Proverbs 14:11-14 (NKJV) The house of the wicked will be overthrown, But the tent of the upright will flourish. There is a way that seems right to a man, But its end is the way of death. Even in laughter the heart may sorrow, And the end of mirth may be grief. The backslider in heart will be filled with his own ways, But a good man will be satisfied from above.

There is a way that seems right. Intellectually it makes sense. Other people seem to confirm that it is right. Common sense tells us that it is right. But, it leads to death. And, if it's the type of death I experienced in my dream- it must be avoided at all costs. A backslider is focused on his own condition, on his own comfort zone while a good man is in tune with the heart of God. His pleasure comes from intimacy with Father God. His pleasure comes from going where God is going, doing what he is doing and feeling what he is feeling. There is no sense of ease in the storm, but there is satisfaction and joy in the presence of God and by being in active agreement with him.

This booklet is a wake-up call to every one of us. Many will be terribly shocked to find themselves separated from God forever.

Matthew 7:21-23 (NKJV) "Not everyone who says to Me, 'Lord, Lord,' shall enter the kingdom of heaven, but he who does the will of My Father in heaven. "Many will say to Me in that day, 'Lord, Lord, have we not prophesied in Your name, cast out demons in Your name, and done many wonders in Your name?' "And then I will declare to them, 'I never knew you; depart from Me, you who practice lawlessness!'

This scripture is in reference to those who would call themselves 'born again Christians'. People who have understood and actually flowed in the power of the Holy Spirit. They understood their heavenly position and earthly authority as they overcame demons. These were your miracle workers.

So what happened?

Jesus reveals two critical keys to salvation-

1. Knowing Jesus- To be received by Jesus we must know Jesus. We must be hungry and intimate. We must ask, seek and knock. The pursuit of great intimacy with our Bridegroom must be intense and continual. It's not about our position, it's about our love. It's about our obedience and union with God in love, in life and in mission.

2. Lawlessness- This issue is addressed further in my book, "Covens In The Church". In my dream, I represented a lawless church, or a lawless person. Someone who maintained control of my own experience. I was focused on what satisfied, on what comforted. I was not alert to the storm or surrendered to a place of radical participation in the moment.

Again, many people will be devastated to find themselves in Hell one day. Many church-goers. Many who prophesy, many who smile when they see their friends, many who live a 'good' life. Why is this? A lack of pursuit of intimacy and the maintenance of control of their experience on the Earth.

The 'sinner's prayer' is one of the most misused evangelism techniques in the church today. This misuse has had devastating results.

The sinner's prayer has become a ticket to hell for countless people. To ever present someone with a guarantee of heaven by simply repeating a prayer is irresponsible. How many people have you met that believe they are going to heaven because they repeated a prayer at an earlier point in their lives? How many of these people have become deeply intimate with their Lover?

Let's dispel something right now- 'salvation' is not primarily about 'making it' to heaven. It's identifying with the Lover of our souls, the maker of the world and coming to a place of agreement. A place of complete surrender.

It's saying, "Yes, I agree that you are God, that you love me, that there is nothing bad in you. You are perfect. You actually died for me. I deserve nothing, and REGARDLESS of my eternal destiny I will choose to love and serve you every moment of my life." All I want on this planet is to spend every moment of my life in passionate union with my Lord and Master and wonderful friend.

Salvation is falling so deeply in love with Jesus that we'll gladly sacrifice everything to spend just a moment with him. God is so great that he lovingly extends this moment with him into an eternity. It's all about being with God.

I have a difficult question for you. I admit it is an imperfect question as it leaves many theological truths hanging in the balance.

It's a question that will never have to be answered, but it does make the idea of salvation for all of us crystal clear.

Here's the question-

If heaven was never guaranteed for you, would you still crave and love Jesus so much that you would give up everything you have on the earth just to spend the next 30-60 years with him in wonderful intimacy?

Of course, when Jesus finds his lovers on the earth, those who have an intense yearning in the depths of their hearts to be with Him, he simply can't wait to spend eternity with them! That's what the cross was all about! It wasn't a ticket to heaven or immunity from hell. It was a model of perfect love in an imperfect and hateful world. That's why he is calling us to carry our cross- it's the evidence of our love and desire for our Bridegroom.

Consider a great and critical bible story that we all know very well:

This story comes right after Jesus was talking about allowing the little children to come to him. He said,

"Let the little children come to Me, and do not forbid them; for of such is the kingdom of heaven."

Why is this? They just wanted Jesus! They wanted to crawl up in his lap! They wanted to embrace him! Now, let's look at the Rich Young Ruler.

> Matthew 19:16-22 (NKJV) Now behold, one came and said to Him, "Good Teacher, what good thing shall I do that I may have eternal life?" So He said to him, "Why do you call

Me good? No one is good but One, that is, God. But if you want to enter into life, keep the commandments." He said to Him, "Which ones?" Jesus said, " 'You shall not murder,' 'You shall not commit adultery,' 'You shall not steal,' 'You shall not bear false witness,' 'Honor your father and your mother,' and, 'You shall love your neighbor as yourself.' " The young man said to Him, "All these things I have kept from my youth. What do I still lack?" Jesus said to him, "If you want to be perfect, go, sell what you have and give to the poor, and you will have treasure in heaven; and come, follow Me." But when the young man heard that saying, he went away sorrowful, for he had great possessions.

Now, consider how this story goes. Someone decides he wants to follow Jesus, yet on his own terms. This person could easily be found going to a vibrant church every Sunday, repeating a sinner's prayer, lifting his hands in worship, leading a small group, witnessing on the streets and owning several bibles.

Remember, the Rich Young Ruler made the choice to follow Jesus. Most any pastor or evangelist would quickly rejoice and lead this man in a prayer. He would fill out a card and would be directed on how to connect in the church.

This scenario plays out day after day after day around the world. Yet, in this story Jesus did not offer a sinner's prayer, a card to fill out or membership in the church. Jesus rejected this man!

This man was what we would call a 'good man'. He kept the commandments.

However, Jesus required more from this man. Jesus will always search the hearts of those who wish to follow him. In the end of this sad story, Jesus literally communicated to this man who wanted to be a follower of Jesus that he may not follow! Incredible!

I heard a story of a great revivalist who was preaching in the first night of a week long revival. The anointing was so strong that a man rushed up to the altar to get saved right in the middle of this preacher's message. He wanted to get saved!

The revivalist rebuked him publicly and commanded him to return to his seat.

"You, sir, are not ready to get saved. I have yet to reveal what it will cost you. Come back each night and I will let you know when it is time to respond to the call of Jesus."

Wow! Where is this type of gutsy presentation of the costly Gospel today?

I often hear of salvation as a 'free gift'. I completely understand the point that people who use that phrase are trying to get across, but I believe it can have damaging affects to those who are responding to it when it's repeated without explanation. The reality is that salvation is very costly to every one who receives it.

The point is that we did not have the ability to 'get saved' on our own. We were not able to control the situation and do anything in ourselves to get saved. Jesus loved us so much that he did it all. He did what we could not do and extended his 'free gift'.

> Romans 6:22-23 (NKJV) But now having been set free from sin, and having become slaves of God, you have your fruit to holiness, and the end, everlasting life. For the wages of sin is death, but the gift of God is eternal life in Christ Jesus our Lord.

The free gift of eternal life must be responded to. We become servants and friends of the Most High God. If Jesus' death on the cross was all that was required for salvation, then every person on the earth would be saved. The cost of our own surrender is high and cannot be overlooked. Every one of Jesus' disciples, except John, were martyred, for example. High cost, yet worth it all.

To extend the point, if a sinner's prayer, or a decision to accept Jesus as our Lord and Savior was all that it took, much of what is revealed in scripture would have to be overlooked.

Remember, salvation is all about intimacy with our Bridegroom and not simply a ticket to heaven. Many who receive the 'free gift' of Jesus' death on the cross, and his resurrection from the dead, and who repeat a prayer and make a decision to follow Jesus will end up eternally separated from God.

The story of the Rich Young Ruler demonstrates this.

Jesus will say to many, "Depart from me, I never knew you." For the sake of clarity on this very important subject, allow me to qualify briefly the point that is being made. The argument is that salvation is a very serious issue, and that a casual desire to go to heaven and to take the name of Jesus is dangerous. The qualification is this- God is in charge of who goes to heaven, and his heart cries out for all to be saved.

> 2 Peter 3:9 (NKJV) The Lord is not slack concerning His promise, as some count slackness, but is longsuffering toward us, not willing that any should perish but that all should come to repentance.

He is longsuffering and deeply desires for people to be saved.

We don't work for our salvation, but rather fruit does follow our salvation. Evidences. The bible makes it clear that some who haven't stepped into deep intimacy with Jesus will most definitely make it to heaven. The thief on the cross is probably the best example.

While the Word tells us that those in the church who are lukewarm will be rejected by God, there is quite apparently a type of person who will live a substandard Christian life who will 'make it' to heaven.

> 1 Corinthians 3:14-17 (NKJV) If anyone's work which he has built on it endures, he will receive a reward. If anyone's work is burned, he will suffer loss; but he himself will be saved, yet so as through fire. Do you not know that you are the temple of God and that the Spirit of God dwells in you? If anyone defiles the temple of God, God will destroy him. For the temple of God is holy, which temple you are.

This scripture reveals a very narrow exception for people whose fruit is proven to be lacking and unacceptable. This person will be saved- but barely. The scripture goes on to clarify the serious nature of eternal life. It's not a simple matter, nor a light matter. If we destroy God's temple, we will be destroyed. If we reveal inappropriate fruit, we may still be saved. But, if our work endures, and our temple is pure, salvation is a guarantee.

We can be confident in our eternal position, though I often find myself crying out to God something like, "Father, my heart longs for intimacy with you. I know I fail so often. I know I choose comfort over you at times. Please, Lord, help me ensure that you and I remain intimate. We remain in love. I don't take your relationship or your salvation lightly. I know it's possible to lose that relationship and that salvation. Help me surrender all, take up my cross and excitedly follow you. I love you."

Note that in that prayer I don't reveal my fear of 'missing heaven'. My fear is losing intimacy with Jesus. Of course, I don't want to go to hell and I don't want to miss heaven- but that's not my motivation. Our focus must be on the wonderful relationship with Jesus that we will either enjoy or lose sight of in our day-to-day experience on this planet.

The churches in the book of Revelation reveal great truths in regard to the serious nature of salvation. God was not pleased with all of their works. In fact, in Revelation chapter 3 we see it revealed that names can be removed from the Book of Life.

> Revelation 3:5 (NKJV) "He who overcomes shall be clothed in white garments, and I will not blot out his name from the Book of Life; but I will confess his name before My Father and before His angels.

If we overcome, our name is securely kept in the Book of Life. If we do not overcome, our name which was written in that Book at the time of our salvation will be blotted out.

Salvation is serious stuff.

I'll share another experience that, I strongly believe, was critical in securing my relationship with Jesus. I believe a negative response to what the Lord was speaking to me would have put my eternal position at jeopardy. Would I have lost my salvation? I don't know and I don't want to play with that fire.

I knew that once saved, everything changed. A great barometer of salvation is to ask whether everything in our lives was open for change or not. I know that once saved, God would begin to change me and require much from me.

2 Corinthians 5:17 (NKJV) Therefore, if anyone is in Christ, he is a new creation; old things have passed away; behold, all things have become new.

Additionally, I understood that simply agreeing that Jesus was God wasn't enough to be saved. I had to surrender all.

Acts 10:43 (NKJV) "To Him all the prophets witness that, through His name, whoever believes in Him will receive remission of sins."

This scripture does not indicate that all we have to do is have some belief that Jesus existed, and that he died and rose from the dead. Even the devil believes that! The word 'believes' literally means, "to be committed to", or "to commit oneself to". It's an all out surrender to the Living God.

Now, on to another life changing experience with God.

This happened shortly after I had the terrifying dream in the old church building. God was wildly challenging me and drawing me closer to him. I was in my early twenty's at the time. Our church, along with several others in the area participated in a 'lock-in' at a local YMCA. There were a few hundred people there enjoying everything from wally-ball to basketball to ping-pong.

They had set up a prayer room in one part of the building. As a young man who was getting blasted by the Holy Spirit with amazing regularity I presumed the room would be full of hungry young men and women of God. Sadly, I was wrong, though the nearly empty room provided me quite an atmosphere to pray in.

In many ways, that room was similar to the one in my dream. I was looking out of the windows over the city as I spent some time with the Lord. However, unlike the dream, I was passionately enjoying God with intensity. The atmosphere was full of the presence of the Holy Spirit. It was literally one of the most powerful 'God moments' of my life. I was so full of life that I found myself pacing around with lifted hands for a long time.

All of a sudden, I 'heard' something in my spirit.

"John, I want you to give me permission to take your life."

Huh? Where in the world did that thought come from? What an unwelcome interruption it was! I shook it off and moved back into prayer and worship. But, something was wrong. The warm and consuming presence of God had left the room. I didn't realize it then, but God's presence didn't leave the room- it had simply changed. God was honoring me with a serious call to follow Him.

I tried for the next 15 minutes to enter back into prayer, but I felt entirely alone. No unction, no flow, no passion.

I kept hearing the words, "John, will you let me take your life?"

I finally realized that the warmth of God's presence had transitioned into the challenge of God's purposes. He was testing me. Was I really ready to take up my cross?

I honestly thought, beyond any doubt, that the decision I was about to make to my Lord would result in my death that very night.

But, I couldn't stand to live the rest of my life outside of the warmth of the tangible presence of Jesus.

"God, if it will result in warming your heart, and in advancing your Kingdom on the Earth, you can take my life. I love you and you are teaching me more about love in this moment than in my previous two decades. I trust you."

The split second I said that in my heart, the fire of the Holy Spirit rushed in with power. It was better than any previous experience with God I had ever had. I was consumed by his love. I was surrendered to him unlike anytime in my life. I was his.

To this day I don't know if God will suddenly take my life- and while I wish to live for a long time on earth, I am longing to live for eternity with my Lover.

Calls from the heart of God like this one come to me from time to time. How serious am I? Am I 'in it' for the benefits? Do I live my life for what I can get out of it? Or, am I a walking dead man? The positive response to the call of God is an indicator of the intimate love that we have for our Lover. It is a fruit of our salvation.

THE BAROMETER OF PRAYER

I have many barometers in my life. I am an imperfect man who loves to discover lack in my life. That discovery leads me on an adventure of pursuit and acquisition of the new things of God for me. For example, if I don't easily heal the sick, then I am thrilled to read books, study the Word of God, watch teachers on TV and pray a lot so I can grow in this gift.

I believe an absolutely critical barometer for any follower of Jesus is that of prayer. Prayer is simply 'being with God'.

I shared a moment ago about my experience in the prayer room in the YMCA. It was nearly empty. I remember another time during that year just after a youth worship service. I was experiencing God so dramatically and so continually that I was probably glowing in the dark! I went outside after that service, and with a goofy smile on my face, told some of my new friends just how amazing God is.

"Wow! Guys, God is so amazing! Whoa! His anointing and his fire is powerful! I can't imagine ever living without him!"

These guys, whom I would pray with on a regular basis, just looked at me with a half smile and said something like, "John, that's great. Yep, God's good."

Where was the passion for Jesus? The explosion of emotion that I was experiencing?

Each Thursday night for one hour prior to the youth service there was prayer in the sanctuary. They heavily announced the prayer meeting, put signs on the doors, talked with people one-on-one and ensured the prayer was the most emphasized portion of the entire night.

Week after week between 60-100 young people would arrive early- and stand outside of the sanctuary in the foyer. The large sanctuary looked empty as 5-6 zealots pressed into the presence of God for one hour and the small foyer looked like a fire hazard as it was jammed to its limits.

You may be saying, "Well, John, many of those young people may not even be saved. They were just babes in the Lord at best."

Ok, that may be true. Let me ask a question- how many times have you seen a similar scenario take place with adults?

I talked to someone just the other day regarding prayer. She stated that her church of about 500 people is resistant to the idea of prayer. The prayer room in the church had 6 chairs in it. It was then moved from the second floor to the third floor, and in the process removed 3 of the chairs. How can this be?!

There is a GREAT SIN of prayerlessness in this nation! Prayer is simply 'being with God'. Intimacy must follow salvation and prayer is the vehicle of intimacy. I'll never understand why the call to intimately be with God in prayer is countered with excuses and no-shows. It literally breaks my heart.

I don't know how often I've heard people respond to the call to the prayer room with excuses like:

- I am always in prayer- in the car, while doing dishes, at work.
- God is with me wherever I go.
- God knows my heart and my needs. I trust he'll take good care of me.

The fact that we attempt to validate non-aggressive, passive and non-costly methods of prayer above the wonderful experience of spending hours of hungering and groaning as the Holy Spirit breathes through us in the prayer room reveals a tragic crisis in the Church!

We should not be making excuses for not being with Jesus!

There is a difference between being in the omnipresence of God and being in the manifest presence of God. Everybody is in God's omnipresence. Satanists, witches, children, adults, preachers and sinners.

it costs much to press into God's manifest presence. It takes time, effort and passion. Period. God is drawing us into the Holy of Holies, yet we have become satisfied with the outer courts!

There is a difference between passively praying throughout our day and actively pressing into God's presence. We must discover God's heart in prayer. We talk a lot about 'lengthy prayer' at Revolution House of Prayer. It is absolutely non-negotiable. We have an event called Prayer in the Cave. We crawl into a deep cave, turn out the lights and 'be with God'.

It takes usually an hour of laying in perfect silence before our hearts are at a place of being invaded by the Holy Spirit. Repentance takes another long season. Worshipping and crying out to God takes more time. Then, finally, we can hear God. We wait and wait as the prophetic Word of God is delivered to us. Then, and now it's been 3-4 hours, we are ready to enforce what's on God's heart. We war in the Spirit and experience wildly enjoyable and effective prayer. Our love of God is intense, our passion is hot and the outcome is amazing. People who experience this wouldn't trade it for anything! Excuses aren't made to avoid prayer, but instead declarations are made to friends, family and our own calendars that we have an appointment with God that will not be violated!

Let me say this clearly- people who are saved simply crave to be with their Lover- Jesus. Lengthy prayer is an obvious reality for them as they understand the many issues of life that must be contended with in order to enjoy God freely.

Does that mean everybody is 'glowing in the dark' and full of life and fire every moment of their lives? Does it mean that prayer isn't hard work sometimes? Of course not! It also doesn't assume that everybody has tangibly experienced God- but those who love God, whether they have experienced him or not, will do whatever it takes to experience him initially and then over and over again.

God needs us to be with him intimately and continually. Much of that time will be passive- while we are in the car or cleaning the house- and much will be very active. I consider the following passage of scripture to be one of the saddest in scripture. Its story was also indicative of things to come.

> Matthew 26:42-44 (NKJV) Again, a second time, He went away and prayed, saying, "O My Father, if this cup cannot pass away from Me unless I drink it, Your will be done." And He came and found them asleep again, for their eyes were heavy. So He left them, went away again, and prayed the third time, saying the same words.

The saddest phrase is, "He left them."

At history's most critical moment, Jesus was craving intimacy with his friends, and when he found none, he went to be with his Father, alone. He had something to accomplish, so while he didn't leave them in terms of his friendship with them, he did leave them when it came to partnering, or the lack thereof, in purpose.

Our desire to be with God will be maintained through thick and thin. God has much to do, and he is calling his lovers to be with him as he does it. Our love of Jesus will keep us awake and alert. The disciples wanted to experience very passive prayer (it is very possible to sleep in the Spirit!) while Jesus was calling them to the most active prayer of their lives. When they didn't respond, Jesus left them.

I know some may quote a scripture at this point, which is one of my favorites:

> Matthew 11:28-30 (NKJV) "Come to Me, all you who labor and are heavy laden, and I will give you rest. "Take My yoke upon you and learn from Me, for I am gentle and lowly in heart, and you will find rest for your souls. "For My yoke is easy and My burden is light."

"But John, God has promised us a light burden. It seems as if you are preaching a very heavy burden when you discuss lengthy prayer."

First of all, let me say this- prayer is wonderfully enjoyable. Those who tap in to the heart of God simply become addicted to lengthy prayer.

But, let's also address the incredibly difficult and important seasons of prayer that require much of us. God's burden in these situations is very light WHEN we enter them in his strength and not ours. God's assignments for us are so heavy and severe that it is completely impossible and burdensome for us to accomplish. Many get very frustrated as they stare God's impossible directives for them in the face.

What's the missing element here? The power of the Holy Spirit that can only be received through being with God! As we are with God intensely and with wild regularity, we will, day-by-day, discover the ability to obey God by carrying the burdens he has given us to carry.

> Romans 8:26-28 (NKJV) Likewise the Spirit also helps in our weaknesses. For we do not know what we should pray for as we ought, but the Spirit Himself makes intercession for us with groanings which cannot be uttered. Now He who searches the hearts knows what the mind of the Spirit is, because He makes intercession for the saints according to

the will of God. And we know that all things work together for good to those who love God, to those who are the called according to His purpose.

We should literally find ourselves in our prayer closets realizing the monumental tasks that God has laid on us, identified our incredible weaknesses and fall on our faces yearning and groaning before the Lord. Many have not allowed the Holy Spirit to physically groan through them. We intercede and cry out and pray in the Spirit day in and day out as we receive the burdens that the Holy Spirit is willing and able to carry through us.

We must hear God's voice so we can know what he wants us to do. We've all heard the scripture that "all things work together for good...", but we miss the point all too often. If we are intimate with God and if we are receiving his purpose for our lives, the heavy burden which is made light through the ministry of the Holy Spirit, things work together for good. If we don't hear God, don't pray, don't receive his burden and aren't intimate with him- things in our lives can be very bad. We must intentionally be with God, hear God, be intimate with God, receive God's ministry and mandates and allow the Holy Spirit to work and groan through us. Our flesh then becomes crucified and our spirits dance and stir as we excitedly move into the realm of the impossible!

Our flesh often tries to determine how much we will carry because it knows how much it can handle. Instead of surrendering to God's plans, we attempt to manage our own burdens. Our tolerance for pain dictates how far we go.

Our flesh tells us how much to pray, how much to fast, how much to serve, how much to give. Our flesh determines the extent of our obedience.

However, when we are 'with God' in the furnace of prayer, we become 'super powered' as the Holy Spirit takes over. We can now obey God and press into the incredible life God has called us to live.

When I started Revolution in 2001, I naively assumed that people who participated with us would see the extreme nature of the vision to take a city for Jesus and would quickly conclude that a radical departure from life as usual must occur. I believed people would get so excited about accomplishing the impossible that they would immediately respond to calls to fast, to pray and to reorder their lives.

After all, the only way to do what God was calling us to do was to be empowered by the Holy Spirit through lengthy prayer. It seemed obvious to me.

God then spoke to me very powerfully, "You must communicate the following message clearly and continually- cares of life must be eliminated!"

Here's the section of scripture that deals with the cares of life:

Luke 8:14-15 (NKJV) "Now the ones that fell among thorns are those who, when they have heard, go out and are choked with cares, riches, and pleasures of life, and bring no fruit to maturity. "But the ones that fell on the good ground are those who, having heard the word with a noble and good heart, keep it and bear fruit with patience.

Those who are inward focused and pursue pleasure and comfort, and who focus on the cares of life, will not mature. I knew a call to take an entire city required people to very quickly respond to this truth regarding the cares of life. It would take serious and maturing people. It couldn't be a long process, but a quick response to press in, pray, fast and reprioritize their lives.

Those who hear the word keep it and bear fruit with patience. It's a radical life.

I believe God is restoring the church to be much like the first church in the Book of Acts. While today church leaders avoid scheduling too many events because of the demands of life on people, we will see these demands finally giving way to the structure God had originally ordained. God's ways will trump life's demands.

> Acts 2:46-47 (NKJV) So continuing daily with one accord in the temple, and breaking bread from house to house, they ate their food with gladness and simplicity of heart, praising God and having favor with all the people. And the Lord added to the church daily those who were being saved.

They were actually at church every day! They also met in homes. A lot of activity with God and other believers was taking place. They had favor and the harvest was large. Can you imagine people today praying in the church every day? Well, it is coming and it will mark the most powerful season the church has ever experienced!

The Lord spoke something to me recently. He told me the Holy Spirit is moving on the face of the earth right now, and he is recruiting. He's recruiting those who will respond to him, and who will participate in a great end time move of God. A great battle. He said that he is not installing a draft. This end time army will be made up of those who are willing and ready- those who discern the signs of the times. Those who resist, some who will still be secure in their salvation and others who won't, will feel the force of the move of God on the earth instead of partnering with God.

God is calling us to surrender all. Many are just cruising along in life, relaxing and doing their best to be comfortable. Many will not make heaven.

Even Billy Graham's own research shows a mere 2% of people who fill out a decision card at one of their evangelistic crusades ever end up pursuing their walk with the Lord.

I've heard of a person who was taken to heaven in 'real time'. They watched as people entered eternity. Some went to heaven, and some went to hell.

A recent Gallup poll reveals that 45% of people in America call themselves 'born again'. On this particular day, this individual reported that only about 2% of the people who died that day entered heaven. While this is not verifiable, it is nonetheless striking. We could deduct fairly reliably that well over 90% of people who had at one time repeated a sinner's prayer, probably attended church and lived a 'good life' were never known by God and ended up in hell.

Intimacy with God is achieved through prayer. I suggest it's a matter of eternal life and death to ensure the prayer rooms of America' churches are full.

Revolution Church was transitioned to Revolution House of Prayer recently. God had spoken clearly to me about the deep importance of having entire cities that pray and worship him 24-hours a day. I decided to contact someone at the International House of Prayer in Kansas City, Missouri. I emailed several questions to them, and one of their leaders responded back to me.

The answer to one question broke my heart and sent flags flying and alarms sounding.

"How do visitors respond when you tell them that the mission of IHOP is to minister to God 24-hours a day in prayer?"

The answer? "They often look back at us with a confused look on their face." I too have experienced this tragic phenomena.

How can this be? How can they be confused? It simply doesn't make sense. Where is the deep longing to be with the Lover of our souls? Where is the lovesick bride?

God's house is a House of Prayer. Period. There is a trend that must be eliminated from our mind-sets- the trend of participating in churches or spiritual activities based on what we can get out of them. Entire churches are set up with the mind set of having the most programs so they can serve the most needs of the most people! When did this happen?

We are called to bring our sacrifices to the altar! We are called to surrender all! To minister to God!

I contend that one of the best things that churches in America can do is to cancel all of their programs, small groups, Sunday School classes and activities- and pray. For a year. Who will stay? Who will thrive? Who will leave? Who will complain?

Can you imagine what this nation and this world would be like if for 365 straight days and nights every single church and every single pastor and every single believer would be in the prayer rooms? Revival would burn across this land and the harvest would be received in world record time!

As it is now, churches call a prayer meeting and the people scatter- America, we have a problem.

A reformation of ministry to the Living God is coming to our land. Churches are abandoning old wine skins and are transitioning to the original intent on God's heart- for his house to be a house of prayer for all nations.

Relationships will be developed in the prayer rooms. We'll go out for coffee after our prayer watches and study the Word together. We'll enjoy each other's company in our homes. We'll live a life of continual prayer, continual growth and continual relationships with other fire-breathing Christians- and it won't be dependent on a program!

What about the lost? I contend that they will finally have a good reason to get saved.

Let's go churches of America- open up the prayer rooms again!

Other Revival Nation books by John Burton

COVENS IN THE CHURCH

During the process of deciding to heed a call of God to move to Colorado, a couple read Covens in the Church. They shared their testimony with me. They reported a great offense crawling up their spine as they read the book. It was hard for them to embrace. Through the process of prayer, they felt God confirming that what they were reading was what they needed to grasp as they were moving on. What they shared next was stunning. They went to their pastor and shared their call to move. However, they told him this, "Pastor, we honor you as our God ordained authority. Though we feel that we are to go, if you feel it is not the right move, we will honor you and stay. It's your call." Tears rolled down the pastor's cheeks. He said, "I've been in ministry for 15 years and you are the first people who have ever asked me to partner with them as they moved on. Thank you."

Other Revival Nation books by John Burton

SIX ENEMIES OF FULFILLED DESTINY

Currently you can find exactly 614,952 "How To..." books on a popular online bookseller. For less than twenty dollars you can learn "How to win friends and influence people," "How to change the world," "How to cheat at everything," "How to be an adult," and even "How to read a book." Planted in all of us at conception is a deep desire to fulfill our purpose on the Earth. Some are consumed by this persistent call to the point of fatigue, anxiety and burnout. Others have tasted the bitterness of defeat and failure and have surrendered any thought of significance. Early in life they may have excitedly read, "How to change the world", but have long since put that book back to collect decades of dust on the bookshelf. Their preferred resources now read more like, "How to get a good night sleep" or "How to escape the pain of failure and rejection." I pray the book in your hands will help reignite the fire of passionate pursuit toward your fulfilled destiny.

ORDER ONLINE AT WWW.JOHNBURTON.NET

Other Revival Nation books by John Burton

REVELATION DRIVEN PRAYER

Listen. Can you hear His voice? What's He saying? Those questions have probably frustrated more people through the ages than we could fathom. Books have been written about unanswered prayer. The walls of pastor's and counselor's offices have soaked up countless quotes like, "I don't hear God". "God doesn't talk to me." "I have no idea what I'm supposed to do". And then, like clockwork, the question is asked to the counselor, "What do YOU think I should do?" After all, to ask that question of someone we can see, and someone who can hear us, not to mention someone who will instantly talk back... audibly... so we can hear clearly and easily... seems to make a lot of sense. Certainly that person has the answers we're looking for, right? Well, sometimes yes, sometimes no.

ORDER ONLINE AT WWW.JOHNBURTON.NET

Other Revival Nation books by John Burton

20 ELEMENTS OF REVIVAL

The contention of this book is simple - THE EXTREME MANIFEST PRESENCE OF GOD IS THE BIBLICAL NORM for a New Testament believer. We label it many ways - revival, an outpouring, renewal - and certainly different moves of God have distinct flavors to them. However, regardless of the descriptive term we attach to it, we simply are not experiencing it. Just as we don't attempt to start driving a car in fifth gear, we should understand that the pursuit of revival must begin at the appropriate place. As we move through the gears, we will find ourselves picking up speed and momentum toward the goal of a city-wide outpouring of the Holy Spirit!

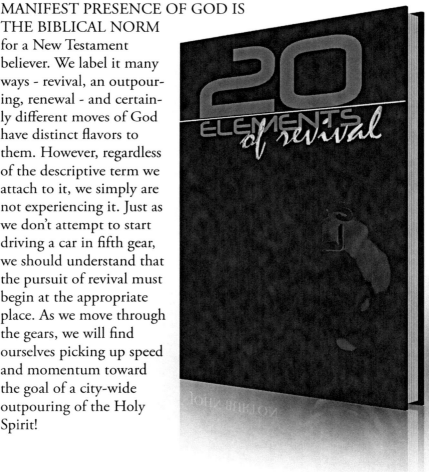

ORDER ONLINE AT WWW.JOHNBURTON.NET

A book by John's wife, Amy Burton

THE SIGNIFICANT LIFE

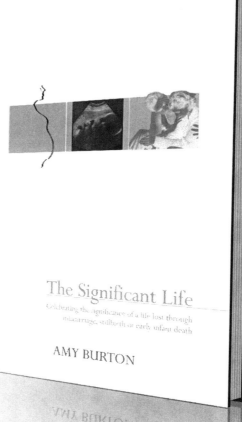

During the lonely weeks and months following the death of their unborn or newly born child, most parents seek to affirm the existence of their baby. Well-intentioned comments such as, "It's for the best," or "You can have another one," minimize the significance of the lost child and suggest that he or she was irrelevant or replaceable. The Significant Life seeks to meet the most basic needs of bereaved parents by validating their grief and celebrating the life of their miscarried or stillborn son or daughter. The Significant Life enables parents to confront their emotions and work toward grief resolution. As the author shares her story of personal loss, she guides the reader toward hope and restoration. Every step of this healing journey commemorates a life that, however brief, has left his or her parents eternally changed.

ORDER ONLINE AT WWW.JOHNBURTON.NET

Printed in the United States
136271LV00003BA/4/P